WRITE AWAY!

POETRY

chartwell
books

> # I never started a poem whose ending I knew. Writing a poem is discovering.
>
> —Robert Frost

Introduction

Since you've picked up this book, no doubt you've fallen in love with a poem at some point in your life. Whether it was a nursery rhyme from childhood or something you read in a high school English class, something about poetry's form has captured your attention. And now you'd like to try writing a poem yourself. But where do you start?

Page through any book of poems and you'll see right away that poets write about all kinds of topics or feelings, and it's no different for you. In fact, from the moment you put pen to paper, you're a poet! And like other poets, your goal is to express yourself in a way that's different from how you would write a short story or even a letter. But for most of us, it's easy to let our inner critic take over and silence our creative voice. Thoughts like "I don't have anything profound to write about" or "where do I start?" or "no one wants to read this!" shut us down before we even begin.

That's where this journal comes in. The 101+ writing prompts and exercises sprinkled throughout will help you find inspiration, try new approaches to writing, and learn to play with language. They'll encourage you to think creatively and look at your world in a new way. Use these prompts to get your creative juices flowing and shut down that inner critic. Remember, this is your journal—there is no right way to follow these prompts. Do them in order or jump around; do one a day or several in a row. These pages are yours for the creating! Then, once you get through the book, challenge yourself by going back and writing new material in response to the prompts to see how your writing has evolved. Maybe you'll find the start of a brand-new poem to fall in love with.

Write a poem about lost or forgotten things.

Make a list of pairs of words (both objects or concepts) that are often paired together. *Ex. salt and pepper, rich and famous.*

dynamic duos

Write a poem about or that includes this idiom: **" miss the boat "**

Make a list of descriptive words to describe a place you'll never go again.

Write a poem about the place you'll never go again.

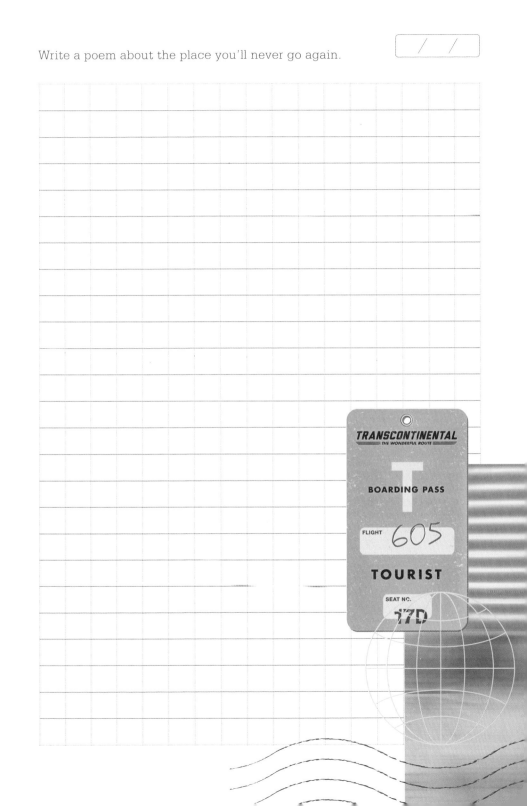

TRANSCONTINENTAL
THE WONDERFUL ROUTE

BOARDING PASS

FLIGHT 605

TOURIST

SEAT NO.
17D

Write an acrostic poem using your name.

an acrostic

is a poem in which the first letter of each
line spells out a word. For example, the first
letter of each line below spells L-O-V-E.

Let me say to you that
One day without you is like a
Very long lifetime. I don't
Ever want to be without you.

Write poems about your pet peeves.

Create a list of alliterative phrases.
Circle ones you like or might want to use in a future poem.

alliteration

is the repetitive use of the same initial
sound in a series of words
(as in *same*, *sound*, and *series*).

Write poems about your favorite smells.

Write a poem that is just a series of questions.

Write a poem about feeling forgotten.

Write a poem about your favorite time of day.

Write a poem about your favorite season.

Find a recent email and use the first line of it to begin a poem.

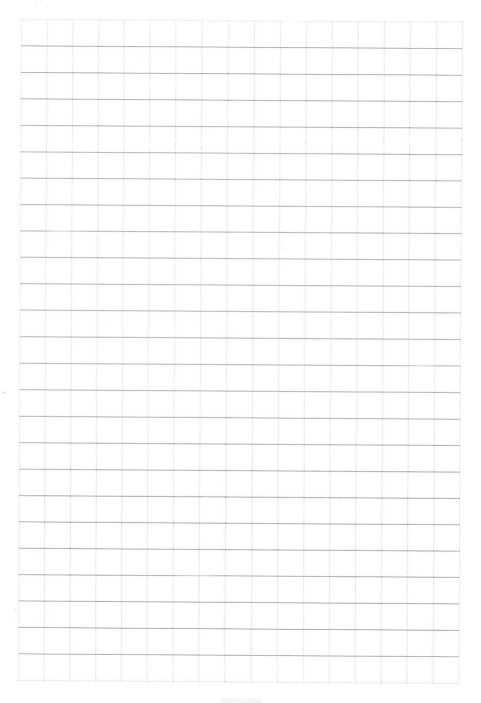

Write a poem that includes elements or scenes from
reoccurring or vivid dreams you have had.

Write poems that would make your grandmother blush.

Write poems from the perspective of your favorite animal.

Write poems about or from the perspective of your favorite fictional character(s).

Write about travelling or places you've travelled.

CABIN BAGGAGE
IN PASSENGER'S
OWN CARE

◁ TRANSPORT SERVICE ▷

03-64-28-84

03642

1$

TRANSPORT SERVICES

Write an acrostic poem using your friend's name.

Write a poem about an embarrassing moment.

Create a list of words you love to say aloud. Do you see any trends?

word play

Write a poem from the perspective of an animal that swims.

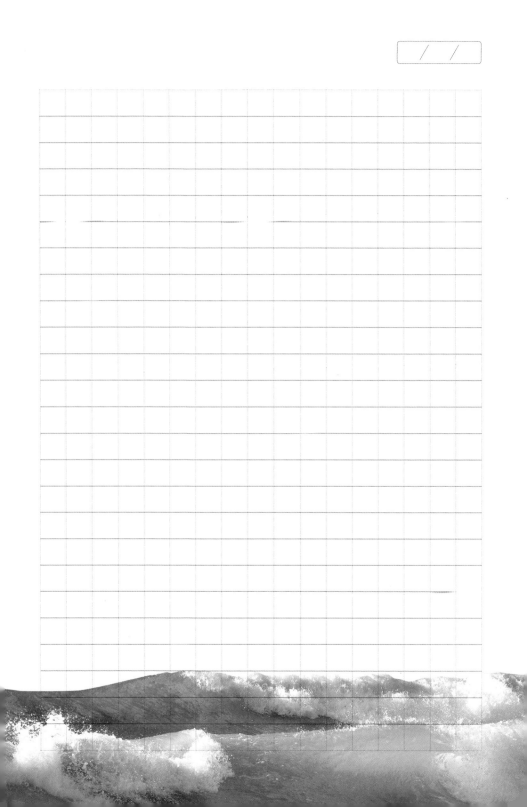

Write a poem about your worst teacher.

Write a poem about or that includes this idiom: **" *it's a piece of cake* "**

Recall an object you saw discarded or being given away on a sidewalk or side of the road. Write the backstory of how it got there.

Write a poem about or that includes this idiom: **"*let the cat out of the bag*"**

Write a poem about or that includes this idiom: **" *it's not rocket science* "**

Think intensely about the color blue. Write down
all images, feelings, and words that come to mind.

Write a poem about or that includes this idiom: **"bite the bullet"**

Play around with the shape your poem takes when written out on the page. Write inside these triangles.

Write a poem that fits inside this circle.

Write a poem about or that includes this idiom: *"time flies when you're having fun"*

Create a list of two-word opposite parings.
Ex. light and dark, win or lose.

Write a poem using four of the two-word pairings.

Play around with the shape your poem takes when written out on the page. Write a poem that fits inside this arc. Does the shape affect the meaning of the poem?

Create a list of words you dislike
(either because of how they sound or what they mean).

word play

Play around with the shape your poem takes when written out on the page. Write poems that fit inside these stars.

Think intensely about the color red. Write down all the images, feelings, and words that come to mind.

Write to an ancestor of yours whom you have never met.

Write down a list of advertising jingles and slogans that come to mind. What about those words make them so vivid or "sticky" in your mind?

Write an over-the-top, cheesy love poem.

Write down some simple sentences. Change the punctuation of the sentences (from period to question mark, exclamation point, ellipsis, etc.) to change the meaning and context.

play with punctuation

"Let's eat Grandma!"

"Let's eat, Grandma."

Write a poem and begin each line with the letter E.

Write a poem about a favorite piece of furniture in your childhood home.

Write a modern nursery rhyme.

Make a list of foreign words you like.

Write out lyrics to your favorite song and circle the most vivid lines or phrases.

Pick one item out of your purse or wallet and write about it.

Eavesdrop on a conversation the next time you're in a public place. Write down overheard sentences or phrases.

Write out your favorite poem from a published poet. Does the act of writing the words deepen or change your feelings about the poem?

Write a poem about your hair.

Write a poem about your hands.

Write a poem about a time you were (or felt) lost.

Write about why you want to write.

Write a poem about an everyday task or mundane chore in a new light.

Write a poem from the perspective of a personified object.

Write a haiku: Pick any topic but limit yourself to the traditional haiku form.

a haiku

is a poem with three lines, with the first
line having five syllables, the second line
containing seven syllables, and the last
containing five syllables.

> A haiku has five
>
> Syllables, then seven, then
>
> Five more at the end.

Write a poem that plays around with onomatopoeia.

onomatopoeia

is a word that sounds like its meaning, such
as *drip*, *sizzle*, or *meow*. Onomatopoeia
comes from the Greek words "onoma" =
name + "poiein" = to make.

Write a poem that plays around with homophones.

Create a list of consonant phrases. Circle ones you like or might want to use in a future poem.

consonance

is the repetitive use of the same consonant sound within
a series of words; it's sort of like rhyming but the sounds
can appear at the beginning, middle, or end of words.
For example, *swish* and *cushion*.

Write a poem in the style of William Shakespeare,
who frequently used iambic pentameter.

_____

_____

_____

_____

_____

_____

_____

_____

_____

_____

_____

_____

_____

_____

_____

_____

_____

_____

_____

_____

_____

iambic pentameter

is a form of meter that emphasizes certain syllables. An
iamb resembles a heartbeat: ba-DUM, ba-DUM, ba-DUM
(think of "To BE or NOT to BE"). Pentameter means there
are five iambs on one line.

Write a poem to your 13-year-old self with advice
for living a good life (or avoiding heartache).

Write a poem to your 70-year-old self with
what you imagine or hope your life will be like.

Write a poem that plays around with personification.

personification

is giving human qualities to non-human creatures or
inanimate objects, for example, "the light danced"
or "the dog laughed at us."

Write a poem in free verse: Pick any topic but don't limit yourself to rhymes, rhythm, punctuation, or rigid stanzas (which are lines of poetry grouped together).

Write a poem using couplets, which are two-line stanzas.

Challenge yourself further by writing a
complete poem in just one couplet!

Shakespeare's famous line from
The Tragedy of Romeo and Juliet is a couplet:

"Good night, good night! Parting is such sweet sorrow

That I shall say good night till it be morrow."

Pick an object in your home and write about it using highly descriptive words. The more mundane the object, the better! Use all your senses when describing the object.

Write a poem from the point of view of the object you
previously wrote a descriptive poem about.

Write a poem about a parent or other parental figure, using only descriptive words or phrases, such as "mustache" and "fishing rods" or "ironing board" and "baking bread."

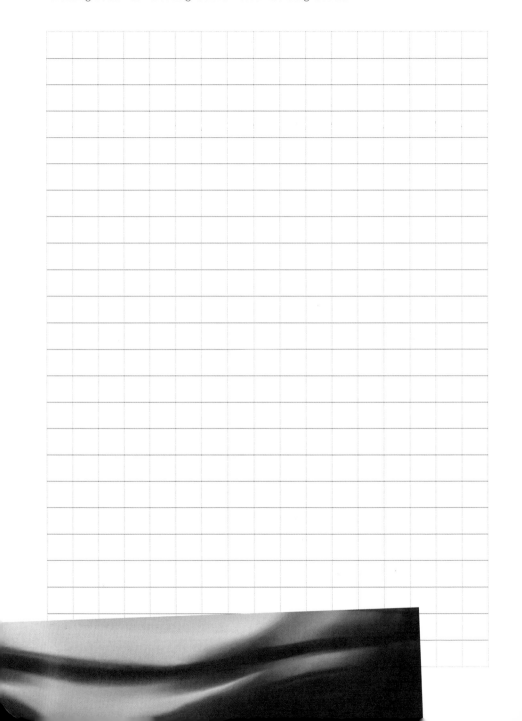

Think of words to describe music you enjoy, then write
a poem using those words to describe something
completely different, like a park or a summer's day.

Write a poem that describes how it sounds when snow, leaves, or rain falls.

Think of words that describe how jumping into a lake on a crisp cold day would feel. Write a poem using those words to describe something completely different, like going on a first date or trying something new.

Write a poem that plays around with anaphora.

_____

_____

_____

_____

_____

_____

_____

_____

_____

_____

_____

_____

_____

_____

_____

_____

_____

_____

_____

_____

_____

_____

anaphora

is the repetition of a word or words at the
beginning of successive phrases or lines. An
example would be Charles Dickens's "It was the
best of times, it was the worst of times...."

Pick your favorite month of the year, and write concrete words that describe it as well as feelings or memories that the month evokes for you.

Write a poem about a red wheelbarrow, expanding on color, shape, setting, and beyond.

Ordinary language communicates information: / /

"The wheelbarrow is red."

poetic language
goes further, conveying senses, emotions, and imagination.
For example, "a red wheel barrow glazed with rain water,"
to paraphrase William Carlos Williams's poem "The Red
Wheelbarrow," could suggest loneliness or hope.

Write an acrostic poem (see page 13) to your parent or grandparent, using their first name.

Write an acrostic poem to your child or pet
(or childhood pet), using their name.

Pick one of your poems in this book and read it out loud (or silently to yourself but deliberately lip-reading, carefully forming each word). How would you change your original poem? Would you add alliteration, alter punctuation, or add a line break? Write a new draft of your poem here.

Let some time pass, then come back to what you rewrote on the previous page. What parts do you consider improved from the original? What parts can be honed further? Try a third draft.

Write a poem that uses multiple denotations of a single word, such as "spring."

denotation

is a word's dictionary meaning; many words have multiple
denotations, like the word "spring," which can mean a
season, a source of water, a coiled wire, or to jump.

Write a poem using scientific language or about science in general.

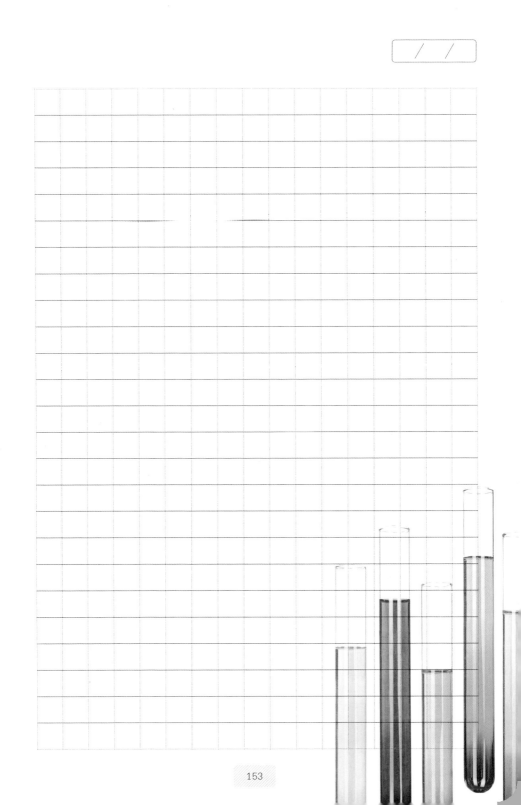

Look or go outside right now and write a poem describing the scene, but rely heavily on imagery.

imagery

is using language to describe what we take in through our senses. For example, on a summer's day, you might *see* blue sky, *smell* a row of blooming honeysuckle, *hear* blue jays screeching, *feel* a cool breeze under the hot sun, and *taste* a ripe raspberry plucked from a bush.

Take the poem you wrote on page 154 and amp up a couple of the descriptions. Is it a *bird*, or it is a *hummingbird*, or is it a *ruby-throated hummingbird*? Is it a *moon*, or is it a *half-moon*, or is it a *yellow half-moon hanging low in the sky*?

Poetry enriches the meaning of words, which is why it can say more with fewer of them. Take one of your previous poems, or write a fresh one here, then look for words you can replace with more meaningful ones based on their connotations. For example, "frigid" instead of "cold," "chariot" instead of "car," or "beloved" instead of "spouse."

connotation

is a word's added meaning or association.
For example, a "doubloon" is just a coin,
but its connotation suggests pirates.

Write a poem about a highly pampered pet, either yours or someone else's.

Write a poem that uses a simile, such as "strong as an ox," "brave like a lion," "as playful as a kitten," "black as coal," "slept like a log," etc.

Write a poem that is not about food or cooking
but written in the form of a recipe.

Write a poem that uses a metaphor, such as "a weight on my shoulder,"
"buried under a sea of melancholy," "house of cards," "heart of stone,"
or "apple of my eye."

_____

_____

_____

_____

_____

_____

_____

_____

_____

_____

_____

_____

_____

_____

_____

_____

_____

_____

_____

_____

_____

_____

a metaphor

is a form of figurative language that compares two things,
but unlike similes, the comparison is more implied rather
than direct. For example, "life is a rollercoaster" compares
the ups and downs of everyday life to those of the much
more thrilling amusement park ride.

Write a poem about a dinner/concert/event you've recently attended.

Write a poem about a dinner/concert/event
you *wish* you could have attended.

Using a previous poem you wrote, try to replace a word
or phrase using synecdoche (e.g., "hit the sheets" means
"going to bed" or "wing" signifies "bird").

To avoid overusing words or
phrases, poets use

synecdoche

which is a literary device where a part signifies the whole;
for example, "new wheels" can mean a new car, "a green
thumb" refers to someone who's good with plants, and
"nice threads" can compliment a pretty outfit.

In the phrase,

"he asks for her hand,"

a man is asking to put an engagement
ring on his beloved's finger; he's not
asking to be given her literal hand.

Write a didactic poem, where you are teaching something or explaining how to do something.

a didactic poem's

primary purpose is to teach and convey a clear message to the reader. Famous didactic poems include "Ulysses" by Alfred, Lord Tennyson, "Still I Rise" by Maya Angelou, and "A Psalm of Life" by Henry Wadsworth Longfellow.

Write a tanka: Pick any topic but limit yourself to the traditional tanka form.

a tanka

is a traditional Japanese poem that is five lines long. The first line and third lines have five syllables and lines two, four, and five have seven syllables, for a total of 31 syllables. Japanese poets historically wrote tanka in one unbroken line.

Using a previous poem you've written, try to replace some of the words using metonymy (e.g., "vintage" instead of "wine," "dish" instead of "dinner," or "ride" instead of "car").

metonymy

is a literary device where a related term substitutes for the thing itself. For example, "the Crown" is largely understood to mean the British monarchy. "The pen is mightier than the sword," means that it is better to communicate ideas (the "pen") than it is to go to war (the "sword").

Write a poem about a childhood memory and include a refrain to signify something that's important or meaningful to you.

a refrain

is a repeated word, phrase, line, or
groups of lines in a poem. Think of any
song on your playlist, where the music
and words repeat periodically.

Write an elegy (a poem of mourning), about the loss of a person or pet, or some other grief you've experienced.

Turn a sentence—any old sentence, from a book, a magazine, an email, or even this one—into a poem. Play around with the form: break it up in different ways, add punctuation, or rearrange the words.

Write out a grocery list or list of errands you need to undertake this week. Now add descriptive or emotional words to the list (e.g., "the reddest apples that are crispy and sweet," "a haircut to give fresh outlook on life," or "a hurried trip to the post office because these cards are late, late, late").

Write a poem about your zodiac sign. (If you don't know it, look it up!)

Write a pangram poem (you can also use a previous poem and alter the words).

a pangram

is a sentence or group of sentences that uses
every letter in the alphabet, as in

*"The quick brown fox jumps
over the lazy dog."*

There once was a man from... Write a limerick!

a limerick
is a five-line poem with an AABBA rhyme scheme that
tells a short comic tale or description of a single subject.

Quarto

This edition published in 2023 by Chartwell Books,
an imprint of The Quarto Group
142 West 36th Street, 4th Floor
New York, NY 10018 USA
T (212) 779-4972 F (212) 779-6058
www.Quarto.com

Contains content originally published as *Write Now!* in 2022 by
Chartwell Books, an imprint of The Quarto Group

10 9 8 7 6 5 4 3 2 1

Chartwell titles are also available at discount for retail, wholesale,
promotional, and bulk purchase. For details, contact the Special Sales
Manager by email at specialsales@quarto.com or by mail at The Quarto
Group, Attn: Special Sales Manager, 100 Cummings Center Suite 265D,
Beverly, MA 01915, USA.

ISBN: 978-0-7858-4342-9

Publisher: Wendy Friedman
Senior Managing Editor: Meredith Mennitt
Senior Design Manager: Michael Caputo
Editor: Jennifer Kushnier
Designer: Kate Sinclair

All stock photos and design elements ©Shutterstock

Printed in China